IT'S TIME TO EAT SALMON

It's Time to Eat SALMON

Walter the Educator

Silent King Books
A WhichHead Entertainment Imprint

Copyright © 2024 by Walter the Educator

All rights reserved. No part of this book may be reproduced in any manner whatsoever without written per- mission except in the case of brief quotations embodied in critical articles and reviews.

First Printing, 2024

Disclaimer

This book is a literary work; the story is not about specific persons, locations, situations, and/or circumstances unless mentioned in a historical context. Any resemblance to real persons, locations, situations, and/or circumstances is coincidental. This book is for entertainment and informational purposes only. The author and publisher offer this information without warranties expressed or implied. No matter the grounds, neither the author nor the publisher will be accountable for any losses, injuries, or other damages caused by the reader's use of this book. The use of this book acknowledges an understanding and acceptance of this disclaimer.

It's Time to Eat SALMON is a collectible early learning book by Walter the Educator suitable for all ages belonging to Walter the Educator's Time to Eat Book Series. Collect more books at WaltertheEducator.com

USE THE EXTRA SPACE TO TAKE NOTES AND DOCUMENT YOUR MEMORIES

SALMON

It's time to eat, what should we do?

It's Time to Eat

Salmon

Let's get some salmon, fresh and new!

It's pink and tasty, good to eat,

A yummy treat, a fishy feat!

We start with a plate, so nice and clean,

A shiny fork, all bright and keen.

The salmon's cooked, it smells so sweet,

A perfect dinner, what a treat!

Sizzle, sizzle, the fish is hot,

Golden brown, it's in the pot.

The fish is flaky, soft, and mild,

Just like a snack for a hungry child.

Add some veggies, green and bright,

Carrots and peas, oh what a sight!

The colors dance, the smells all mix,

A perfect meal, the very fix!

It's Time to Eat

Salmon

Let's take a bite, so tasty and neat,

The salmon's flavor can't be beat!

Juicy, savory, flaky, too,

Yum, yum, yum, it's good for you!

Dip it in sauce, a creamy way,

To make the salmon even more fun today!

Lemon or butter, sweet or tart,

The taste of salmon fills my heart.

We chew and chew, the meal is done,

It was so good, oh what fun!

With full bellies, we smile wide,

We ate some salmon, side by side!

So when you're hungry, what should you seek?

Salmon's the answer, tasty and sleek.

For lunch or dinner, breakfast too,

It's Time to Eat
Salmon

Salmon is healthy, and good for you!

Now it's time to clean up fast,

The meal was yummy, but not to last.

Put the dishes away with care,

Thank you, salmon, we'll see you there!

Tomorrow we'll eat, or maybe soon,

Some salmon again, morning or noon!

So remember, my friend, when it's time to eat,

It's Time to Eat
Salmon

Salmon's the food that can't be beat!

ABOUT THE CREATOR

Walter the Educator is one of the pseudonyms for Walter Anderson. Formally educated in Chemistry, Business, and Education, he is an educator, an author, a diverse entrepreneur, and he is the son of a disabled war veteran. "Walter the Educator" shares his time between educating and creating. He holds interests and owns several creative projects that entertain, enlighten, enhance, and educate, hoping to inspire and motivate you. Follow, find new works, and stay up to date with Walter the Educator™ at WaltertheEducator.com

www.ingramcontent.com/pod-product-compliance
Lightning Source LLC
LaVergne TN
LVHW052014060526
838201LV00059B/4035